The Ten Commandments in Poems

The Ten Commandments in Poems

RONALD E. HIGNITE

RESOURCE *Publications* • Eugene, Oregon

THE TEN COMMANDMENTS IN POEMS

Resource Publications
An Imprint of Wipf and Stock Publishers
199 W. 8th Ave., Suite 3
Eugene, OR 97401
www.wipfandstock.com

ISBN 13: 978-1-62032-389-2
Manufactured in the U.S.A.

The Scripture quotations contained herein are from the King James Version of the Bible.

In loving memory of Len and Carol Hignite,
my Christian father and mother

Contents

Foreword
Preface

Introduction to the Ten Commandments 1

The First Commandment 2

The Second Commandment 5

The Third Commandment 6

The Fourth Commandment 9

The Fifth Commandment 10

The Sixth Commandment 13

The Seventh Commandment 14

The Eighth Commandment 17

The Ninth Commandment 18

The Tenth Commandment 21

Closing to the Ten Commandments 22

Foreword

RONALD E. HIGNITE DEMONSTRATES in *The Ten Commandments in Poems* his poetic skills and provides greater understanding and meaning of God's laws for mankind. Readers will be inspired by the manner and design by which the events at Mt. Sinai are described in poetry and rhyme.

Pastor Gene Williams
Greenville, North Carolina

Preface

It was my pleasure writing *The Ten Commandments in Poems*. I was inspired to write this book following the personal satisfaction I received in composing my previous book, *The Beatitudes in Poems*. The book contains 12 poems with one on each of the Ten Commandments along with an introductory and closing poem. Each poem is accompanied by a religious picture or nature scene. *The Matthew Henry Commentary* was used as a resource for the interpretation of Scripture.

The Ten Commandments or laws for man were proclaimed by God to Moses and his children at Mount Sinai around 1440 BC. The Israelites had been taken out of Egypt and out of bondage by Moses. They are recorded in the Bible in Exodus 20: 3-17 and are the living laws for man's conduct in this life. Jesus, himself, set the perfect example in following these commandments in his own life and expressed them in his teachings to the people. When Jesus was asked about the way to eternal life, he said, "If thou wilt enter into life, keep the commandments." (Matthew 19:17)

Just as the Beatitudes from Jesus Christ's Sermon on the Mount gave man guidelines for the heart to follow in life, the Ten Commandments from God give man ethical standards to follow. I hope these poems will be a blessing to its readers.

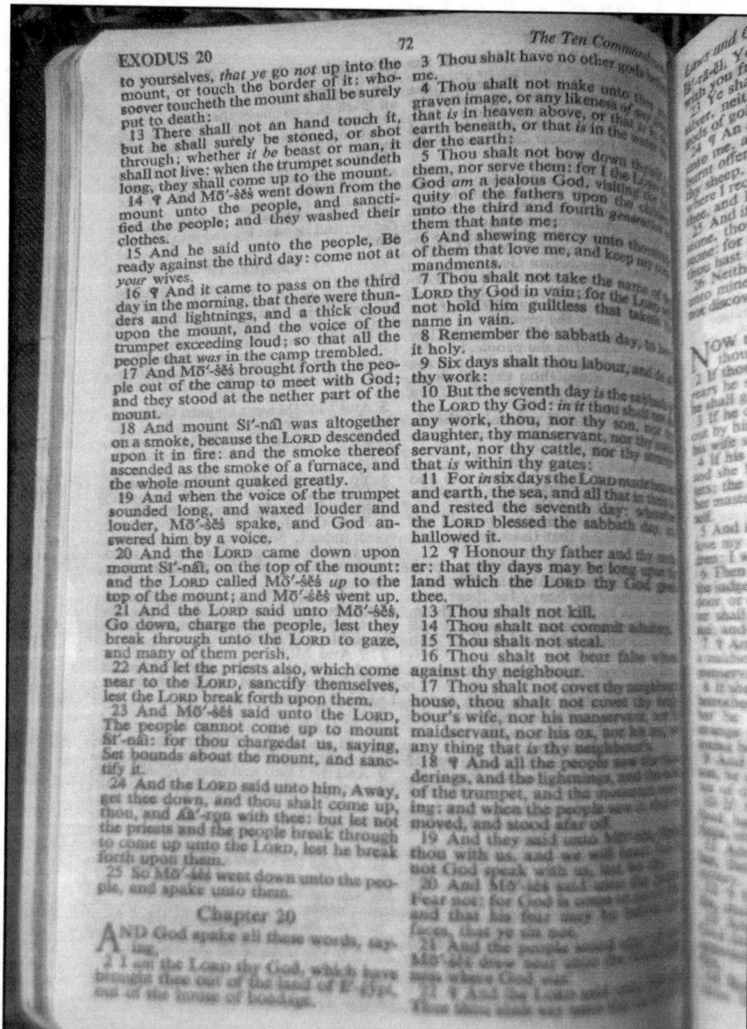
EXODUS 20 72 The Ten Command...

to yourselves, that ye go not up into the mount, or touch the border of it: whosoever toucheth the mount shall be surely put to death:

13 There shall not an hand touch it, but he shall surely be stoned, or shot through; whether it be beast or man, it shall not live: when the trumpet soundeth long, they shall come up to the mount.

14 ¶ And Mō'-šĕš went down from the mount unto the people, and sanctified the people; and they washed their clothes.

15 And he said unto the people, Be ready against the third day: come not at your wives.

16 ¶ And it came to pass on the third day in the morning, that there were thunders and lightnings, and a thick cloud upon the mount, and the voice of the trumpet exceeding loud; so that all the people that was in the camp trembled.

17 And Mō'-šĕš brought forth the people out of the camp to meet with God; and they stood at the nether part of the mount.

18 And mount Sī'-nāi was altogether on a smoke, because the LORD descended upon it in fire: and the smoke thereof ascended as the smoke of a furnace, and the whole mount quaked greatly.

19 And when the voice of the trumpet sounded long, and waxed louder and louder, Mō'-šĕš spake, and God answered him by a voice.

20 And the LORD came down upon mount Sī'-nāi, on the top of the mount: and the LORD called Mō'-šĕš up to the top of the mount; and Mō'-šĕš went up.

21 And the LORD said unto Mō'-šĕš, Go down, charge the people, lest they break through unto the LORD to gaze, and many of them perish.

22 And let the priests also, which come near to the LORD, sanctify themselves, lest the LORD break forth upon them.

23 And Mō'-šĕš said unto the LORD, The people cannot come up to mount Sī'-nāi: for thou chargedst us, saying, Set bounds about the mount, and sanctify it.

24 And the LORD said unto him, Away, get thee down, and thou shalt come up, thou, and Aâ'-ron with thee: but let not the priests and the people break through to come up unto the LORD, lest he break forth upon them.

25 So Mō'-šĕš went down unto the people, and spake unto them.

Chapter 20

AND God spake all these words, saying,

2 I am the LORD thy God, which have brought thee out of the land of Ē'-gypt, out of the house of bondage.

3 Thou shalt have no other gods before me.

4 Thou shalt not make unto thee any graven image, or any likeness of any thing that is in heaven above, or that is in the earth beneath, or that is in the water under the earth:

5 Thou shalt not bow down thyself to them, nor serve them: for I the LORD thy God am a jealous God, visiting the iniquity of the fathers upon the children unto the third and fourth generation of them that hate me;

6 And shewing mercy unto thousands of them that love me, and keep my commandments.

7 Thou shalt not take the name of the LORD thy God in vain; for the LORD will not hold him guiltless that taketh his name in vain.

8 Remember the sabbath day, to keep it holy.

9 Six days shalt thou labour, and do all thy work:

10 But the seventh day is the sabbath of the LORD thy God: in it thou shalt not do any work, thou, nor thy son, nor thy daughter, thy manservant, nor thy maidservant, nor thy cattle, nor thy stranger that is within thy gates:

11 For in six days the LORD made heaven and earth, the sea, and all that in them is, and rested the seventh day: wherefore the LORD blessed the sabbath day, and hallowed it.

12 ¶ Honour thy father and thy mother: that thy days may be long upon the land which the LORD thy God giveth thee.

13 Thou shalt not kill.

14 Thou shalt not commit adultery.

15 Thou shalt not steal.

16 Thou shalt not bear false witness against thy neighbour.

17 Thou shalt not covet thy neighbour's house, thou shalt not covet thy neighbour's wife, nor his manservant, nor his maidservant, nor his ox, nor his ass, nor any thing that is thy neighbour's.

18 ¶ And all the people saw the thunderings, and the lightnings, and the noise of the trumpet, and the mountain smoking: and when the people saw it, they removed, and stood afar off.

Introduction to the Ten Commandments

Moses took God's children
Out of Egypt years ago
For the Israelites were in bondage
As we have come to know.

In the third month of their journey
To Mount Sinai Moses led,
And it was there God made a covenant
With his children as we've read.

As the trumpet sounded,
God shouted out his Word,
And from the smoke and fire
The people trembled at what they heard.

He said he was the Lord thy God
Who had made them free,
And then he proclaimed to everyone
What he expected from them to see.

He delivered his commandments,
His laws for all mankind,
So there would be no question
In anybody's mind.

The First Commandment

"Thou shalt have no other gods before me."

—Exodus 20:3

The first and great commandment,
God declared for all to hear,
And with the lightening flashing
The people listened to him in fear.

It was there upon Mount Sinai
His first commandment came to be.
There Moses and his people heard,
"Thou shalt have no other gods before me."

Jesus reinforced these words
As all the world would find.
"Thou shalt love the lord thy God
With all thy soul, and with all thy mind."

We're not to worship idols
Nor traditions made of men.
Instead, God said to put him first
And to worship others would be a sin.

Since God has truly made you,
Let his will for you be done.
Put God first in all you do
As did on earth his Son.

The Second Commandment

"Thou shalt not make unto thee any graven image,
or any likeness of any thing that is in heaven above,
or that is in the earth beneath, or that is in the water
under the earth."

—EXODUS 20:4

The second commandment then was heard
As God to all did speak.
He told them they must worship him,
And his Spirit they must seek.

"Thou shalt not make unto thee any graven image,"
God said to all back then.
Nothing representing him
Shall be worshipped here by men.

For God is truly limitless
Through his power and his love,
And images only limit
The worship of God above.

For those who worship false gods,
And traditions man might make,
God will cause them havoc
For these measures that they take.

We must learn to walk with God,
And follow him each day.
We must truly worship him
For there's no other way.

The Third Commandment

"Thou shalt not take the name of the Lord thy God in vain."

—Exodus 20:7

The third commandment God proclaimed
For all his children to attain,
"Thou shalt not take the name
Of the Lord thy God in vain."

God must be respected
For he's the Creator of all things.
He's made the heavens and the earth,
And he's the King of kings.

His name should be revered
For it stands for strength and might.
He's the source of all power,
And in this we can't lose sight.

For those who curse the name
Of the One who gave them breath,
God will not take kindly
On those persons after death.

His love and kindness and his mercy
All represent his name,
And we must each respect it
Which has always been his aim.

The Fourth Commandment

"Remember the Sabbath day, to keep it holy."

—Exodus 20:8

"Remember the Sabbath day, to keep it holy,"
God said to all mankind,
And this would be the fourth commandment
That he placed upon our mind.

God made all things in six days
As the Bible said,
And on the seventh day he rested
And blessed it as we've read.

In the footsteps of his Father,
Christ, too, would come along,
And said God had made the Sabbath
For man to rest and worship on.

The Sabbath has been given
To man from God above
For spiritual rededication
And a time to share his love.

So rejoice in the Sabbath,
The day God made for you.
Remember to keep it holy,
And worship on it, too.

The Fifth Commandment

"Honour thy father and thy mother
that thy days may be long upon the land
which the Lord thy God giveth thee."

—Exodus 20:12

The fifth commandment God revealed
For all the world to know,
And it would set the groundwork
Where our reverence for God should go.

He said, "Honour thy father and thy mother
That thy days may be long,"
And to God it was important
That his message be carried on.

We must honor and respect
Our parents every day
For until a child develops
They guide his life in every way.

Jesus Christ would show his love
For his own mother, too.
On the cross for his dear mother
He told his disciple what to do.

We should always honor
Our parents from our birth,
And this same honor should be given
To God our Father while we're on earth.

The Sixth Commandment

"Thou shalt not kill."

—Exodus 20:13

As the thunder sounded,
God shouted out his will,
And gave to all his sixth commandment,
"Thou shalt not kill."

The giver of life is God,
And only God can take it away.
So when someone murders,
God will make him pay.

Hate and anger will destroy
The hearts and minds of men,
And since they cause one to murder,
Christ said they also were a sin.

There have been so many wars
That have broken God's law, too.
Senseless killings have taken place
Against what God would have us do.

God's coming will end all wars,
And no more killing will be found
For God's law of love will flourish,
And peace and calmness will abound.

The Seventh Commandment

"Thou shalt not commit adultery."

—Exodus 20:14

The seventh commandment then came forth,
And it was loud and clear,
"Thou shalt not commit adultery,"
God said for all to hear.

God made a woman for a man
To make his life complete,
And adultery will destroy
And make the union weak.

Adultery wrecks a marriage,
And it wrecks the family, too.
The children are so hurt
From what their parents do.

Marriage is a sacred thing
As God has let us know,
And he desires commitment
From each of us to flow.

Marriage was ordained by God,
And this law we must obey.
To commit adultery in this life
For us is not God's way.

The Eighth Commandment

"Thou shalt not steal."

—Exodus 20:15

"Thou shalt not steal,"
God shouted as before,
And this would be the eighth commandment,
And there would be two more.

Man's property is his own,
And another shall not take it,
And God would make this law
Strictly for man's own benefit.

There are many forms of theft
That now go on today.
False advertising is just one
That steals from those who pay.

Man should also not rob from God
That which he should give.
Tithes and offerings should go out
To God from all who live.

Man shall not take from others
What does not belong to him,
And on Mt. Sinai God made it clear
To everyone of them.

The Ninth Commandment

"Thou shalt not bear false witness against thy neighbour."

—Exodus 20:16

"Thou shalt not bear false witness
Against thy neighbour," God spoke out to all,
And his ninth commandment would be shared
By his followers like Paul.

Man should live by truth
As found within God's Word,
And this truth shall set man free
Like many now have heard.

Lies by man have poisoned us,
And they occur most every day.
These lies and false teachings trick us
Through man's deceptive way.

Dictators and politicians, too,
They tell us what we want to hear.
Then when they're in power,
They set policies we fear.

Respect is gained for man
In what we see him do.
So if you live a life that's truthful,
Respect will come to you.

The Tenth Commandment

"Thou shalt not covet thy neighbour's house, thou shalt not covet thy neighbour's wife, nor his maleservant, nor his maidservant, nor his ox, nor his ass, nor any thing that is thy neighbour's."
—Exodus 20:17

"Thou shalt not covet thy neighbour's house,"
God then disclosed to them.
"Nor any thing that is thy neighbour's,"
It was said to all by him.

We must learn the way of God,
And the things that he would do
For our hearts they should be pure
Filled with love and joy, too.

We will not find a peace of mind
In covetousness and lust.
The reward is only temporary
If it's not in God we trust.

A bigger car, a bigger house,
They're often lusts not needs.
They bring to us financial woes
That to depression leads.

His tenth commandment made it clear
That to covet was a sin,
And true fulfillment in man was found
By serving God within.

Closing to the Ten Commandments

Yes it was there upon Mount Sinai
In the desert years ago
Where God would make a covenant
With his people for all to know.

The Ten Commandments that you've read
God gave to all mankind
That they become the living laws
That live within each mind.

Jesus Christ would come along
Sent by God above,
And he would magnify these laws
Through his obedience and love.

Christ set the perfect example
For all the world to see.
He taught and followed these commandments
And desires the same for you and me.

As recorded in the Book of Matthew,
Christ would make it clear
That man should follow these commandments
For the time that he is here.

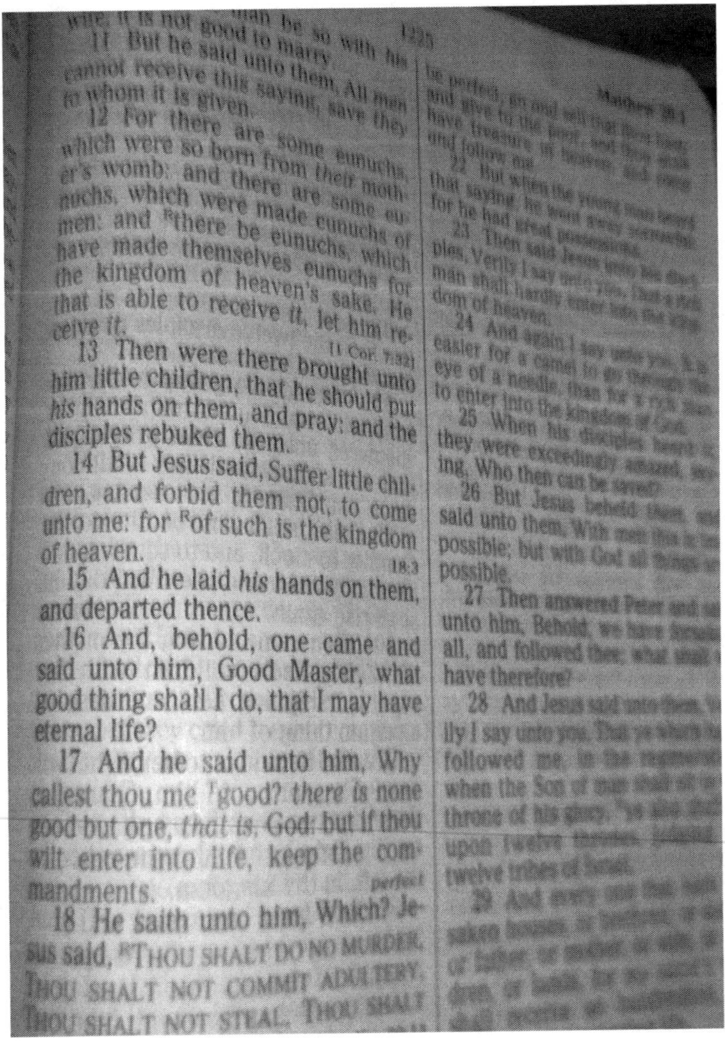

wife, it is not good to marry.
11 But he said unto them, All men
cannot receive this saying, save they
to whom it is given.
12 For there are some eunuchs,
which were so born from *their* moth-
er's womb: and there are some eu-
nuchs, which were made eunuchs of
men: and there be eunuchs, which
have made themselves eunuchs for
the kingdom of heaven's sake. He
that is able to receive *it*, let him re-
ceive *it*.
13 Then were there brought unto
him little children, that he should put
his hands on them, and pray: and the
disciples rebuked them.
14 But Jesus said, Suffer little chil-
dren, and forbid them not, to come
unto me: for of such is the kingdom
of heaven.
15 And he laid *his* hands on them,
and departed thence.
16 And, behold, one came and
said unto him, Good Master, what
good thing shall I do, that I may have
eternal life?
17 And he said unto him, Why
callest thou me good? *there is* none
good but one, *that is*, God: but if thou
wilt enter into life, keep the com-
mandments.
18 He saith unto him, Which? Je-
sus said, THOU SHALT DO NO MURDER,
THOU SHALT NOT COMMIT ADULTERY,
THOU SHALT NOT STEAL, THOU SHALT